Level 1

THE OLDER BEGINNER PIANO COURSE

by James Bastien

The Bastien Older Beginner Piano Library

PREFACE

The **OLDER BEGINNER PIANO COURSE** leads the student step by step through basic keyboard fundamentals. Each book contains original music and carefully selected familiar music to provide an enjoyable learning experience. A functional approach is used allowing the student to play and harmonize melodies from the beginning. Multi-key reading is introduced gradually through the course.

For optimum results the **OLDER BEGINNER, LEVEL 1** is designed to be used simultaneously with its companion book **MUSICIANSHIP, LEVEL 1.** Theory, technic, and sight reading materials are presented comprehensively in this book.

Complete materials designed to be used in conjunction with this book are listed below.

FLIP

Published by Kjos West.
Distributed by Neil A. Kjos Music Company.
National Order Desk, 4382 Jutland Dr., San Diego, CA 92117

ISBN 0-8497-5029-6
Cover Photo: Harry Crosby/Photophile

CONTENTS

UNIT 1

- **THE PIANO KEYBOARD**
- **THE MUSICAL ALPHABET**
- **FINGER NUMBERS**
- **RHYTHM IN MUSIC**
- **C MAJOR FIVE FINGER POSITION**
- **THE C CHORD**

THE PIANO KEYBOARD

The piano keyboard has black and white keys. The black keys are grouped in sets of twos and threes.

Tones sound higher when you play to the right on the keyboard (up the keyboard), lower when you play to the left on the keyboard (down the keyboard).

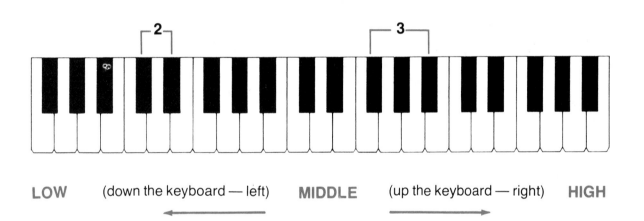

LOW   (down the keyboard — left)   MIDDLE   (up the keyboard — right)   HIGH

PRACTICE DIRECTIONS	1. Play all the sets of two black keys. Play the low keys with your Left Hand, the high keys with your Right Hand. 2. Play all the sets of three black keys. Play the low keys with your Left Hand, the high keys with your Right Hand.

You are ready to begin a new book in the **OLDER BEGINNER PIANO LIBRARY — Musicianship, Level 1.**

THE MUSICAL ALPHABET

The Musical Alphabet names the white keys on the keyboard.
The same seven letters (A, B, C, D, E, F, G) are used over and over.

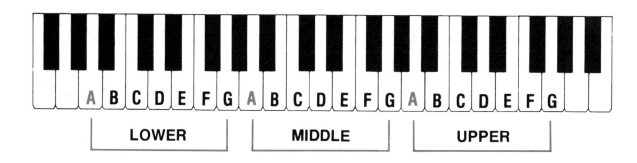

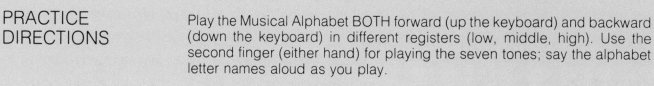

| PRACTICE DIRECTIONS | Play the Musical Alphabet BOTH forward (up the keyboard) and backward (down the keyboard) in different registers (low, middle, high). Use the second finger (either hand) for playing the seven tones; say the alphabet letter names aloud as you play. |

Individual white key names are found in relationship to the black keys.

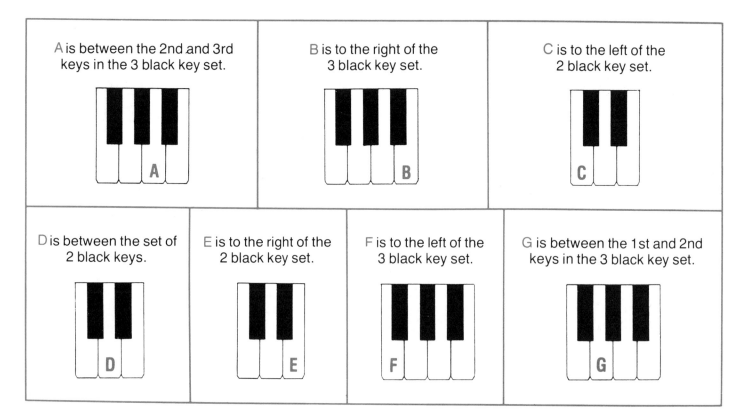

A is between the 2nd and 3rd keys in the 3 black key set.

B is to the right of the 3 black key set.

C is to the left of the 2 black key set.

D is between the set of 2 black keys.

E is to the right of the 2 black key set.

F is to the left of the 3 black key set.

G is between the 1st and 2nd keys in the 3 black key set.

| PRACTICE DIRECTIONS | Locate and play individual white keys. Use the second finger (either hand). MEMORIZE the location of each key name. |

FINGER NUMBERS

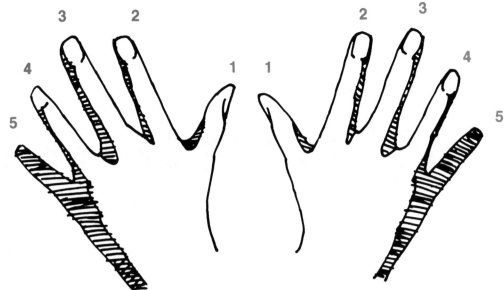

LEFT HAND (L.H.)   **RIGHT HAND (R.H.)**

PRACTICE DIRECTIONS	Say these finger numbers aloud, moving the corresponding fingers up and down. Learn these finger numbers so they become automatic.

RHYTHM IN MUSIC

Every piece has a pattern of short and long tones. The combination of short and long tones is called RHYTHM.

QUARTER NOTE	♩ (one clap) Count: "quarter" or Count: 1	HALF NOTE	♩ (clap - shake) Count: "half - note" or Count: 1 - 2

PRACTICE DIRECTIONS	Clap and count the following note values aloud. Use either counting system.

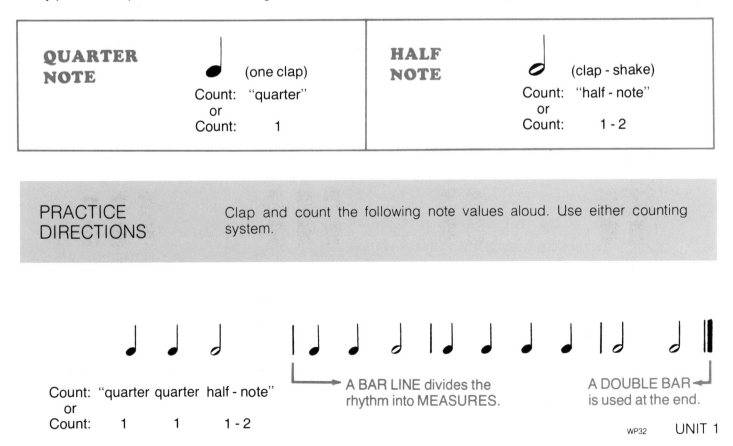

Count: "quarter quarter half - note"
or
Count: 1   1   1 - 2

A BAR LINE divides the rhythm into MEASURES.

A DOUBLE BAR is used at the end.

C MAJOR FIVE FINGER POSITION

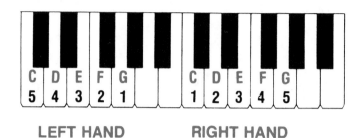

LEFT HAND　　**RIGHT HAND**

- Keep a good hand position when playing the piano. CURVE YOUR FINGERS. Play each key with the tip of your finger.

- When reading music, KEEP YOUR EYES ON THE BOOK.

- Play with a LEGATO touch. Connect the tones smoothly.

PRACTICE DIRECTIONS	1. Clap and count the rhythm aloud aloud before playing. 2. Find the position for BOTH hands. 3. Play and sing the FINGER NUMBERS aloud. (Play the first line with your Right Hand, the second line with your Left Hand.) 4. Play again and COUNT the rhythm aloud. 5. Play again and SING the letter names of the notes aloud.

Warm-Up

Position: C

WHOLE NOTE

𝅝 (clap - shake - shake - shake)
Count: "Whole - note - hold - it"
or
Count: 1 - 2 - 3 - 4

PRACTICE DIRECTIONS

Follow the same PRACTICE DIRECTIONS given on page 8 for these two pieces.

MERRILY WE ROLL ALONG

AU CLAIR DE LA LUNE

Follow the same PRACTICE DIRECTIONS given on page 8 for these two pieces.

THE C CHORD

A CHORD is three or more notes played at the same time.

The C chord is formed from three of the keys in the C Major Five Finger Postition. Usually chords are played with the Left Hand to form HARMONY to accompany melodies.

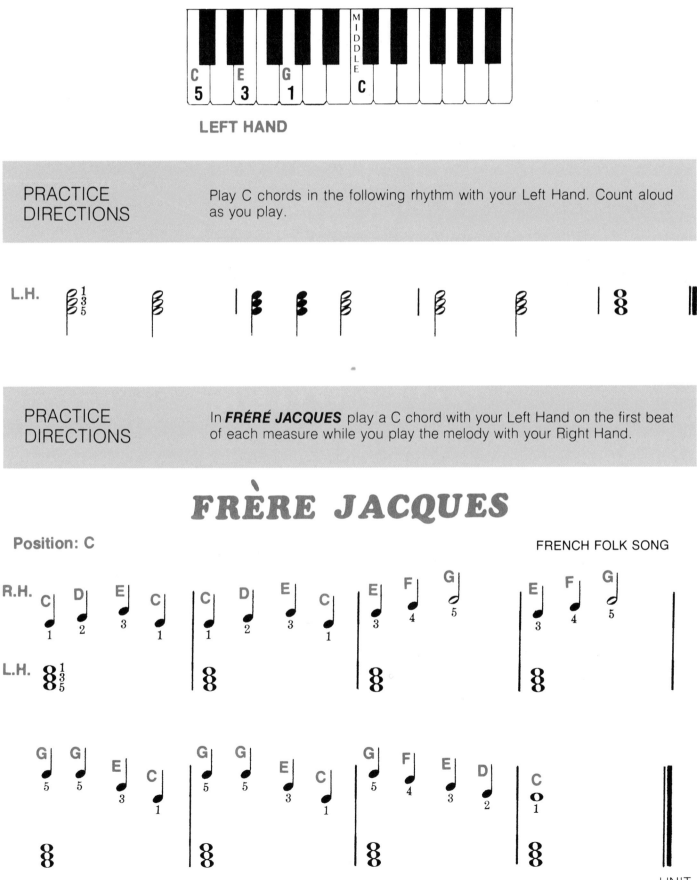

LEFT HAND

PRACTICE DIRECTIONS	Play C chords in the following rhythm with your Left Hand. Count aloud as you play.

PRACTICE DIRECTIONS	In **FRÈRE JACQUES** play a C chord with your Left Hand on the first beat of each measure while you play the melody with your Right Hand.

FRÈRE JACQUES

Position: C

FRENCH FOLK SONG

REVIEW · UNIT 1

1. Write the letter name of each key marked with an X.

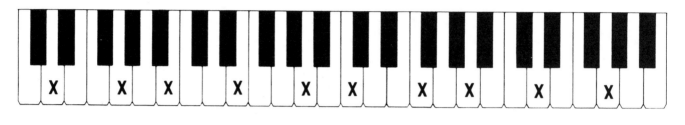

___ ___ ___ ___ ___ ___ ___ ___ ___ ___

2. Write the letter names of the keys in the C Major Five Finger Position for both hands.

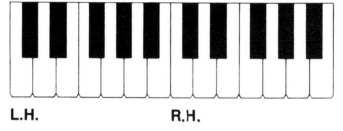

L.H.   **R.H.**

3. Clap and count this rhythm pattern.

4. Write the letter names of the keys in the C chord.

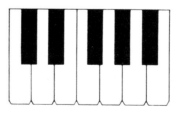

5. Play C chords in the following rhythm with your Left Hand. Count aloud as you play.

UNIT 2

- BEGINNING MUSIC FACTS
- C MAJOR FIVE FINGER POSITION (NOTATION)
- I, V7 CHORDS IN C MAJOR

BEGINNING MUSIC FACTS

STAFFS · CLEFS

The STAFF has 5 lines and 4 spaces.

The TREBLE STAFF is indicated by a TREBLE CLEF (or G clef) sign.

The BASS STAFF is indicated by a BASS CLEF (or F clef) sign.

The Treble Staff and the Bass Staff are joined together by a brace to form the GRAND STAFF.

The note names of the C Major Five Finger Position are shown below. Note that the Treble Clef C is placed on a LEGER LINE (a short line added to the staff to extend the staff).

TIME SIGNATURES

The two numbers written at the beginning of each composition make up the TIME SIGNATURE. The upper number indicates the number of beats (or counts) in a measure. The lower number indicates what kind of a note gets one beat.

$\frac{2}{4}$ 2 beats in each measure $\frac{4}{4}$ 4 beats in each measure

the quarter note (♩) gets one beat   the quarter note (♩) gets one beat

$\frac{3}{4}$ 3 beats in each measure

the quarter note (♩) gets one beat

C MAJOR FIVE FINGER POSITION
(NOTATION)

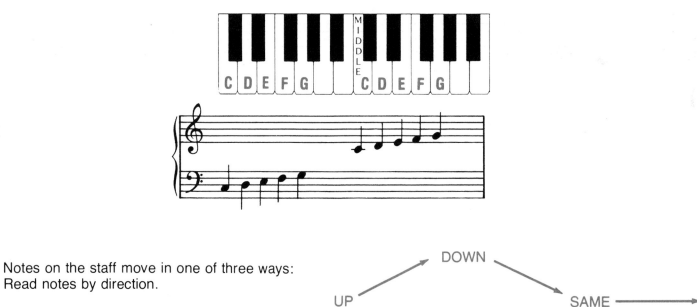

Notes on the staff move in one of three ways:
Read notes by direction.

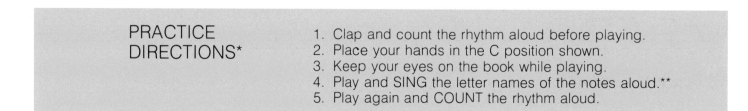

PRACTICE DIRECTIONS*	1. Clap and count the rhythm aloud before playing.
	2. Place your hands in the C position shown.
	3. Keep your eyes on the book while playing.
	4. Play and SING the letter names of the notes aloud.**
	5. Play again and COUNT the rhythm aloud.

Warm-Up

Position: C

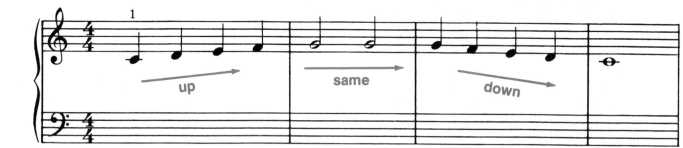

*Similar practice directions should be followed throughout this book.
Drill on these notes using the **Bastien Music Flashcards.

AU CLAIR DE LA LUNE

FRENCH FOLK SONG

FRÈRE JACQUES

FRENCH FOLK SONG

ODE TO JOY

LUDWIG VAN BEETHOVEN

I, V7 CHORDS IN C MAJOR

CHORD PROGRESSION

Changing from one chord to another is called a CHORD PROGRESSION. The I and V7 chords can be used to harmonize many melodies.

Chords are labeled with Roman numerals to indicate the tone of the scale on which each chord is formed.

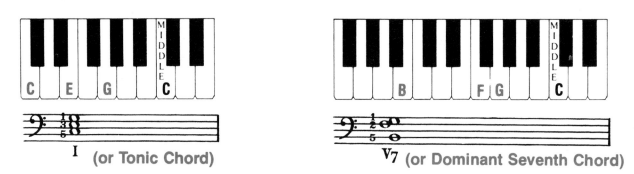

I (or Tonic Chord) V7 (or Dominant Seventh Chord)

Usually chords are played with the Left Hand. To play a V7 chord with your Left Hand, begin with a I chord position. Then:

Keep 1 the same.
Play 2 (in the five finger position).
Move 5 DOWN to the NEAREST key (white or black).

| PRACTICE DIRECTIONS | Practice this Left Hand chord progression in C Major until you can play it smoothly. Play by "feel." Do NOT look at your hand for the chord changes. |

Chord Symbols*

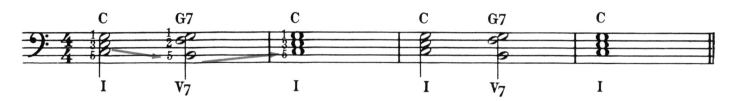

*Chord symbols name specific chords. When chord symbols are printed above melodies, pianists can improvise bass parts. Chord symbols represent a practical form of musical shorthand.

BALANCE OF MELODY AND ACCOMPANIMENT

The melody should always SING above the accompaniment. Play the accompaniment SOFTER than the melody for the correct balance.

TIE	RESTS	NOTES RESTS
A TIE is a curved line which connects notes on the SAME line or space. Play the first note and HOLD it for the combined value of both notes.	RESTS indicate measured silence. Each note has a rest sign of the same value (same number of beats).	**Quarter Rest** (1 beat) **Half Rest** (2 beats) **Whole Rest** (4 beats, or whole measure)

LIGHTLY ROW

Moderately

FOLK SONG

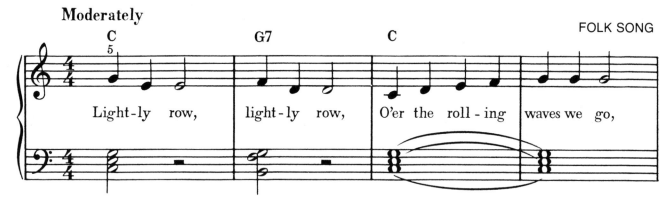

Light-ly row, light-ly row, O'er the roll-ing waves we go,

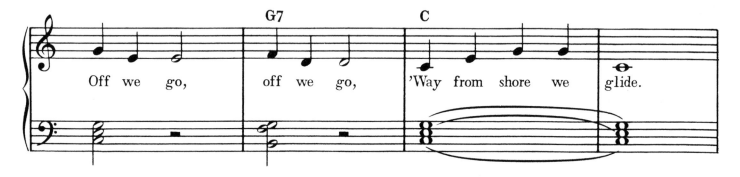

Off we go, off we go, 'Way from shore we glide.

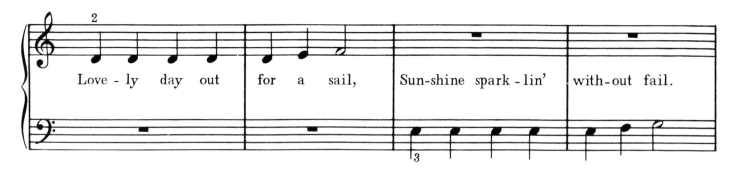

Love-ly day out for a sail, Sun-shine spark-lin' with-out fail.

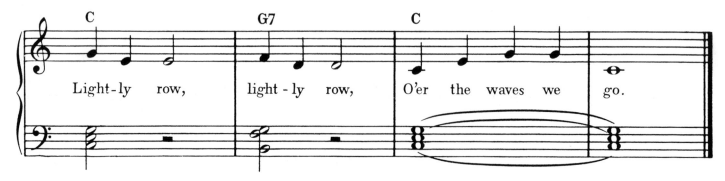

Light-ly row, light-ly row, O'er the waves we go.

DOTTED HALF NOTE	UPBEATS	

DOTTED HALF NOTE

♩. (clap - shake - shake)
Count: "Half - note - dot"
or
Count: 1 - 2 - 3

UPBEATS

Notes which come BEFORE the first full measure of a piece are called UPBEATS. Usually the time value of the upbeat is taken from the final measure, making the final measure INCOMPLETE.

WHEN THE SAINTS GO MARCHING IN

With spirit

TRADITIONAL

Oh, when the Saints go march-ing in,
Oh, when those bells be - gin to chime,

Oh, when the Saints go march - ing in,
Oh, when those Saints bells go be - gin to chime,

Oh, I want to be in that num - ber,
Oh, I want to be in that num - ber,

When the Saints go march - ing in.
When those bells be - gin to chime.

REPEAT SIGNS

The two dots mean to repeat (play again) from the beginning of the piece.

REVIEW - UNIT 2

1. Draw these notes.
   a. Quarter Note   b. Half Note   c. Whole Note   d. Dotted Half Note

   _____   _____   _____   _____

2. A group of 5 lines and 4 spaces is called a _____ .

3. The two numbers written at the beginning of a composition make up the _____ .

4. A curved line which connects notes on the same line [notes] or space [notes] is a

   _____ .

5. Measured silence is indicated in music by _____ .

6. A note (or notes) which comes before the first full measure of a piece is called an _____ .

7. Name these Treble Clef notes. Play them.

   ____   ____   ____   ____   ____   ____   ____

8. Name these Bass Clef notes. Play them.

   ____   ____   ____   ____   ____   ____   ____

9. Play the following chord progression with your Left Hand in the rhythm indicated.

UNIT 3

- **PLAYING OUT OF THE FIVE FINGER POSITION**
- **EIGHTH NOTES**
- **THE IV CHORD**

PLAYING OUT OF THE FIVE FINGER POSITION

MOVING THE THUMB DOWN

Often it is necessary to MOVE YOUR THUMB DOWN to play melodies extending out of the five finger position.

PRACTICE DIRECTIONS	Practice the following exercise as preparation for melodies extending out of the five finger position.

DYNAMICS

DYNAMICS are the degrees of softness and loudness with which music should be performed. Music signs are used as dynamic indicators.

SIGN	ITALIAN NAME	MEANING
p	piano	soft
mp	mezzo piano	medium soft
mf	mezzo forte	medium loud
f	forte	loud

SLUR

A SLUR is a curved line over or under a group of notes. The notes within the slur line are to be played legato (smooth and connected).

MARY ANN

TRADITIONAL

Moderato

All day, all night, Ma - ry Ann, ____

Down by the sea - shore, sift - ing sand; ____

All the lit - tle chil - dren love Ma - ry Ann, ____

Down by the sea - shore, sift - ing sand. ____

EIGHTH NOTES ♪ ♫

An EIGHTH NOTE receives HALF of one beat (in a time signature where a quarter note receives one beat). One eighth note has a FLAG: ♪

TWO EIGHTH NOTES equal one quarter note and receive one beat. Two eighth notes are paired together with a BEAM: ♫

EIGHTH NOTE	EIGHTH REST
♪ = 1/2 beat	𝄾 = 1/2 beat

TWO EIGHTH NOTES

♫ = ♩ (1 beat)

TWO EIGHTH NOTES ♫ (clap, clap)
Count: "Two eighths"
or
Count: 1 and

PRACTICE DIRECTIONS   Clap and count the following rhythm.

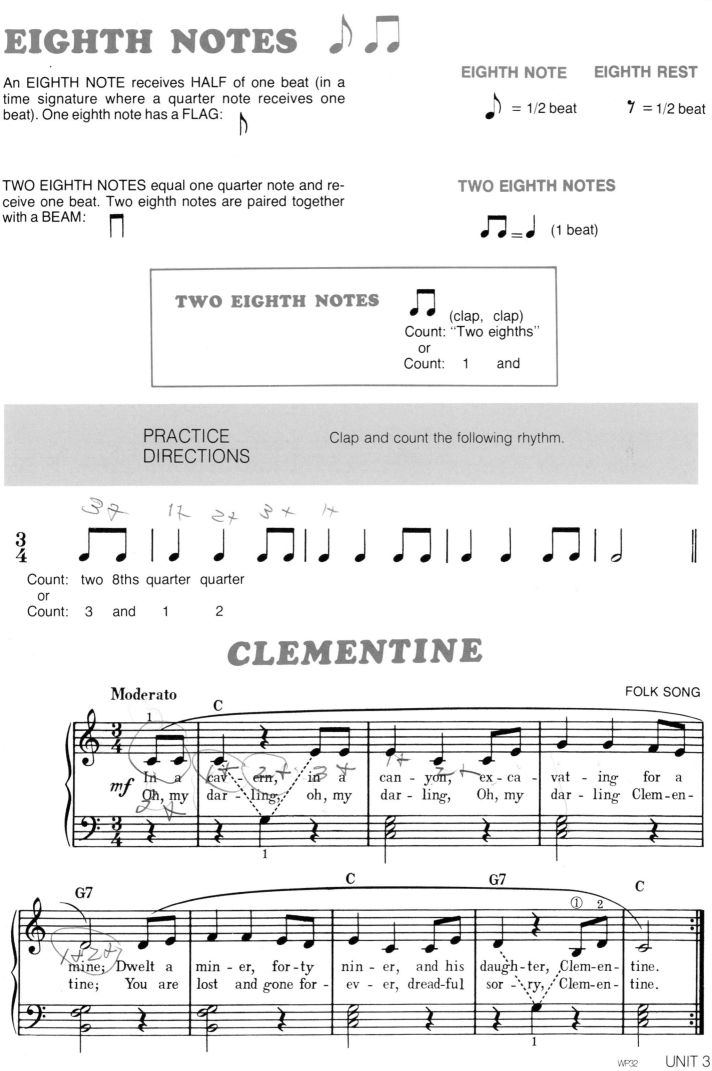

Count: two 8ths quarter quarter
or
Count: 3 and 1 2

CLEMENTINE

Moderato   FOLK SONG

C

In a cav-ern, in a can-yon, ex-ca-vat-ing for a
Oh, my dar-ling, oh, my dar-ling, Oh, my dar-ling Clem-en-

G7   C   G7   C

mine; Dwelt a min-er, for-ty nin-er, and his daugh-ter, Clem-en-tine.
tine; You are lost and gone for-ev-er, dread-ful sor-ry, Clem-en-tine.

THE IV CHORD

By learning the IV chord, you will be able to harmonize many melodies.

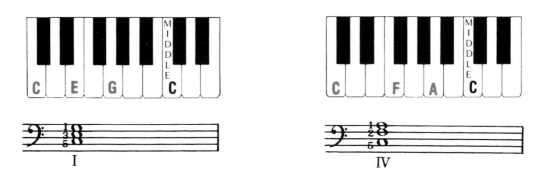

To play a IV chord with your Left Hand, begin with a I chord position. Then:

> Keep 5 the same.
> Play 2 (in the five finger position).
> Move 1 UP TWO keys (black or white).

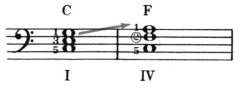

| PRACTICE DIRECTIONS | Practice these Left Hand chord progressions in C Major until you can play them smoothly. Play by "feel." Do NOT look at your hand for the chord changes. |

Chord Progressions

1.

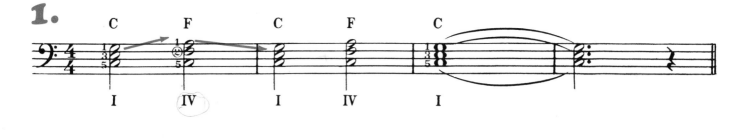

2.

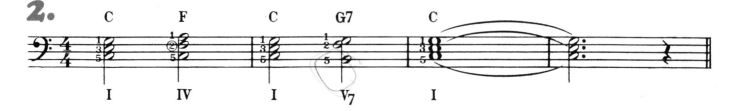

MOVING THE FIFTH FINGER UP

Often it is necessary to MOVE YOUR FIFTH FINGER UP to play melodies out of the five finger position.

PRACTICE DIRECTIONS Practice the following exercise as preparation for melodies extending out of the five finger position.

Preparatory Drill

LAVENDER'S BLUE

Moderato — ENGLISH FOLK SONG

Lav - en - der's blue, dil - ly, dil - ly, Lav - en - der's green,

When I am king, dil - ly, dil - ly, You shall be queen.

Who told you so, dil - ly, dil - ly, Who told you so?

'Twas my own heart, dil - ly, dil - ly, that told me so.

FERMATA SIGN ⌢	**D. C. AL FINE**
This sign is called a FERMATA. It means to HOLD the note (or notes) LONGER than the time value.	*D.C. al Fine* (abbreviation for *Da Capo al Fine*,) is a DIRECTION SIGN. It means to go back to the beginning of the piece and play to the word *"Fine"* (pronounced "fee-nay").

FOR HE'S A JOLLY GOOD FELLOW

ENGLISH SONG

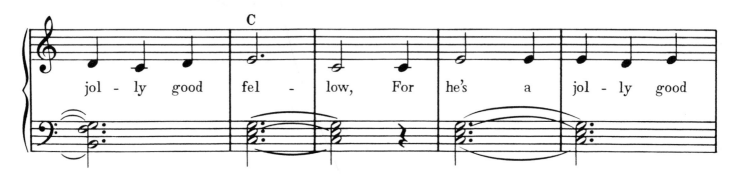

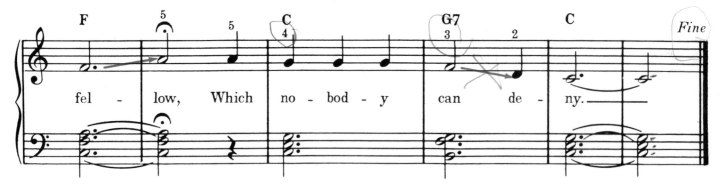

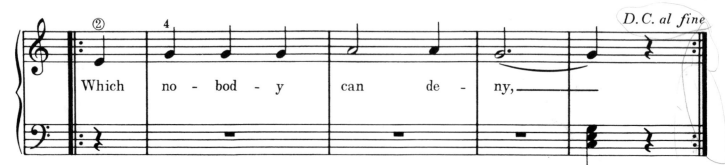

ROCK ABOUT

REVIEW - UNIT 3

1. Draw these notes.
   a. Dotted Half Note   b. Two Eighth Notes   c. Quarter Note

   _____   _____   _____

2. Name these rests.

   _____ _____ _____ _____

3. Name these notes. Play them.

   ___ ___ ___ ___ ___ ___ ___

   ___ ___ ___ ___ ___ ___ ___

4. Draw a note on the staff above each letter. Use whole notes.

   G   Middle C   F   B Below Staff   D   A   E

   D   F   C   A   G   E   D

5. Name these dynamic signs.

SIGN	ITALIAN NAME	MEANING
p	_____	_____
f	_____	_____
mf	_____	_____
mp	_____	_____

6. Play the following chord progression with your Left Hand in the rhythm indicated.

   C F C   C G7 C   C F C   G7   C

UNIT 4

- ACCIDENTALS
- G MAJOR FIVE FINGER POSITION
- I, IV, V7 CHORDS IN G MAJOR

ACCIDENTALS ♯ ♭ ♮

ACCIDENTALS are added signs which temporarily alter the pitch of notes. The effect of accidental signs lasts only within the measure they appear.

A SHARP sign (♯) before a note means to play the NEXT KEY to the RIGHT. The next key may be black or white.

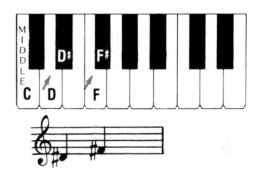

A FLAT sign (♭) before a note means to play the NEXT KEY to the LEFT. The next key may be black or white.

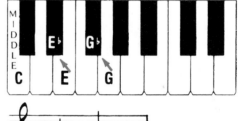

The NATURAL sign (♮) is used to cancel a sharp or flat. It means to play the natural key (white key). Frequently a natural sign is used as a REMINDER in the next measure.

reminder

ENHARMONIC NOTATION

Tones which sound the same but look different in print are termed ENHARMONIC (F♯ = G♭). The English equivalent is "to, too, two."

The keyboard shows the enharmonic names from A to A.

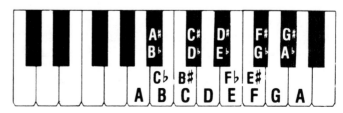

SATURDAY NIGHT

BLUE MOOD

STEPPIN' OUT

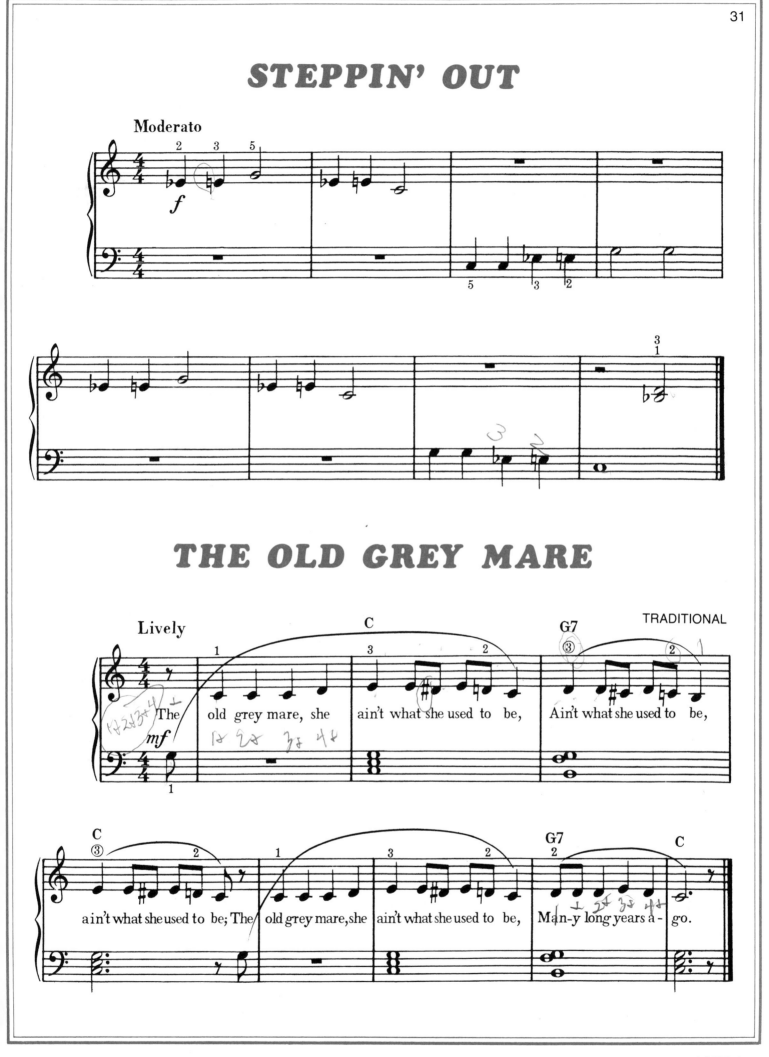

THE OLD GREY MARE

G MAJOR KEY SIGNATURE

The sharps or flats at the beginning of each staff tell you the KEY SIGNATURE. (Exception: the key of C Major has NO sharps or flats.)

The key signature tells you:

1) which notes to play sharped or flatted THROUGHOUT the piece and
2) the main tonality or KEY of the piece..

SHARP KEY SIGNATURES ARE IDENTIFIED BY:
1) naming the last sharp

then 2) naming the next letter in the musical alphabet (the name of the next note ABOVE the last sharp).

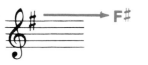

Key of G Major

G MAJOR FIVE FINGER POSITION

PRACTICE DIRECTIONS	Name these notes aloud as you play. MEMORIZE them. *

Warm-Up

Key of G Major

f - p

* Drill on these notes using the **Bastien Music Flashcards.**

MARCH

Steady march tempo

WALTZ

PROMENADE

BUGLES

I, IV, V7 CHORDS IN G MAJOR

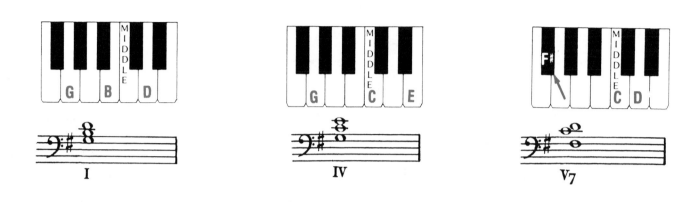

| PRACTICE DIRECTIONS | Practice the following Left Hand **Chord Progression** until you can play it smoothly. Play by "feel." Do NOT look at your hand for the chord changes. |

Chord Progression

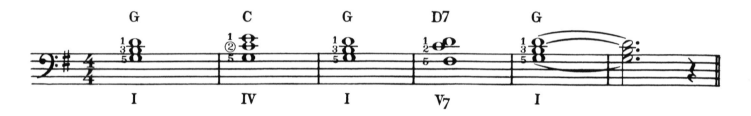

| PRACTICE DIRECTIONS | Practice the following **Preparatory Drill** for balance, playing the Left Hand SOFTER than the Right Hand. |

Preparatory Drill

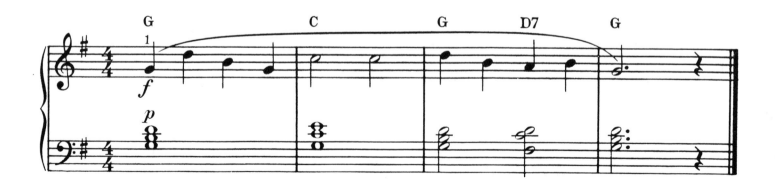

DRINK TO ME ONLY

WORDS BY BEN JOHNSON

ENGLISH SONG

AT SUNSET

REVIEW - UNIT 4

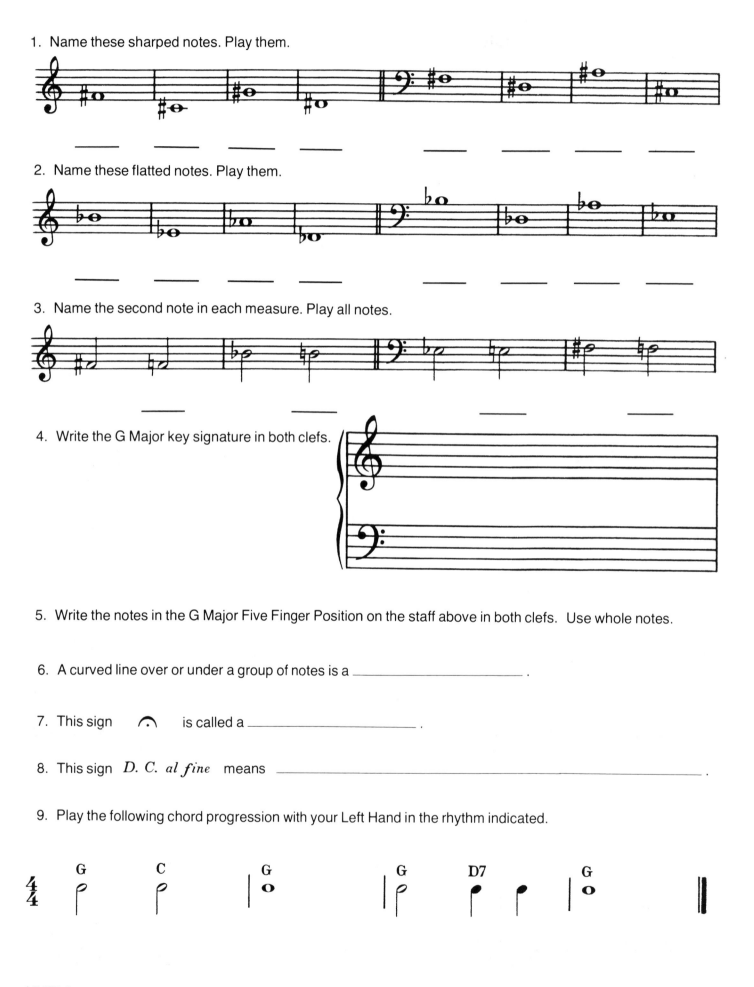

1. Name these sharped notes. Play them.

____ ____ ____ ____   ____ ____ ____ ____

2. Name these flatted notes. Play them.

____ ____ ____ ____   ____ ____ ____ ____

3. Name the second note in each measure. Play all notes.

____ ____ ____   ____ ____ ____

4. Write the G Major key signature in both clefs.

5. Write the notes in the G Major Five Finger Position on the staff above in both clefs. Use whole notes.

6. A curved line over or under a group of notes is a _____ .

7. This sign ⌒ is called a _____ .

8. This sign *D. C. al fine* means _____ .

9. Play the following chord progression with your Left Hand in the rhythm indicated.

UNIT 5

- **F MAJOR FIVE FINGER POSITION**
- **I, IV, V7 CHORDS IN F MAJOR**
- **TRANSPOSITION**
- **DOTTED RHYTHM**

D. S. AL FINE

D. S. al Fine (abbreviation for *Dal Segno al Fine*) is a DIRECTION sign. It means to go back to the sign (𝄋) and play to the word *"Fine."*

THINKIN' 'BOUT YOU

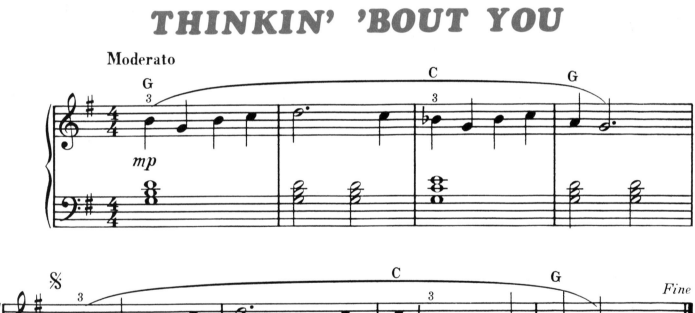

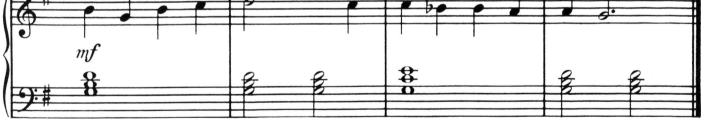

F MAJOR KEY SIGNATURE

The key of F Major has one flat: B flat. In a piece with an F Major key signature, play all the B's flatted.

F MAJOR FIVE FINGER POSITION

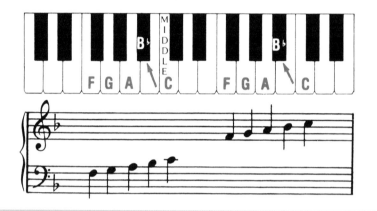

| PRACTICE DIRECTIONS | Name these notes aloud as you play. MEMORIZE them.* |

Warm-Up

Key of F Major

* Drill on these notes using the **Bastien Music Flashcards.**

©1969 GWM, INC., San Diego, California. (Ed. No. GP27)

CHIMES

FOLK DANCE

BELLS

WALTZ

I, IV, V7 CHORDS IN F MAJOR

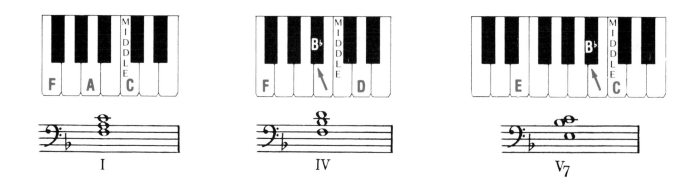

| I | IV | V₇ |

| PRACTICE DIRECTIONS | Practice the following Left Hand **Chord Progression** until you can play it smoothly. Play by "feel." Do NOT look at your hand for the chord changes. |

Chord Progression

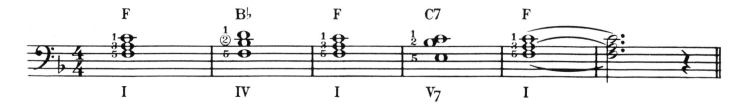

| PRACTICE DIRECTIONS | Practice the following **Preparatory Drill** for balance, playing the Left Hand SOFTER than the Right Hand. |

Preparatory Drill

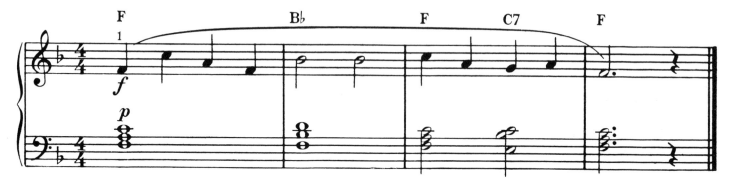

EVENING SONG

TRANSPOSITION

TRANSPOSITION is the process of playing or writing music in a different key from that in which it was originally written.

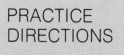

PRACTICE DIRECTIONS	*EVENING SONG* is written below in G Major and in C Major as examples in transposition. First, play the melody in each key; then add the harmony. Repeat several previously learned pieces and transpose them into other keys.

DOTTED RHYTHM ♩. ♪

The rhythm of a QUARTER-DOT EIGHTH figure is a DOTTED RHYTHM pattern. Clap and count this dotted rhythm pattern in the following manner:

Count: "quarter - dot eighth"

or

Count: 1 - and - 2 and

This rhythm has a LONG — SHORT feel.

PRACTICE DIRECTIONS   Clap and count the following rhythm aloud.

PRACTICE DIRECTIONS   Many songs use this dotted rhythm pattern; several are given below. Sing and clap the rhythm to these songs BEFORE playing. Then play each song, counting the rhythm aloud.

LONDON BRIDGE

Lon - don Bridge is fall-ing down, fall-ing down, fall-ing down.

DECK THE HALLS

Deck the halls with boughs of hol - ly, Fa-la-la-la-la - la - la - la - la!

AMERICA

My coun - try, 'tis of thee, Sweet land of lib - er - ty, Of thee I sing.

ALL THROUGH THE NIGHT

MICHAEL, ROW THE BOAT ASHORE

REVIEW · UNIT 5

1. Write the F Major key signature in both clefs.

2. Write the notes of the F Major Five Finger Position on the staff above in both clefs. Use whole notes.

3. Name the Major key shown by each key signature.

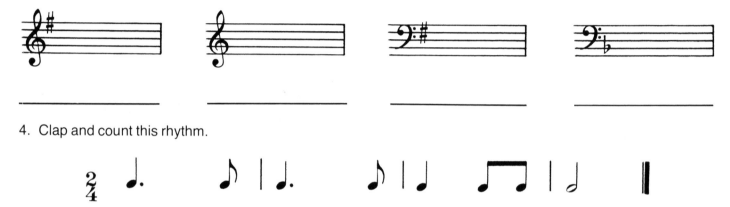

_____   _____   _____   _____

4. Clap and count this rhythm.

5. Play this melody. Count aloud as you play. Transpose it to the keys of G and C.

6. Play the following chord progression with your Left Hand in the rhythm indicated.

UNIT 6

- **STACCATO TOUCH**
- **GROUP 1 KEYS (CHORDS)**
- **GROUP 1 KEYS (FIVE FINGER POSITIONS)**

STACCATO TOUCH

A DOT above or below a note means to play it detached (short, separated). This is called STACCATO touch. Staccato is the OPPOSITE of legato.

PRACTICE DIRECTIONS	Play the following exercise with a staccato touch. Play first with your Right Hand, then with your Left Hand. Play the Left Hand eight notes (one octave) LOWER than written. Play forward and backward.

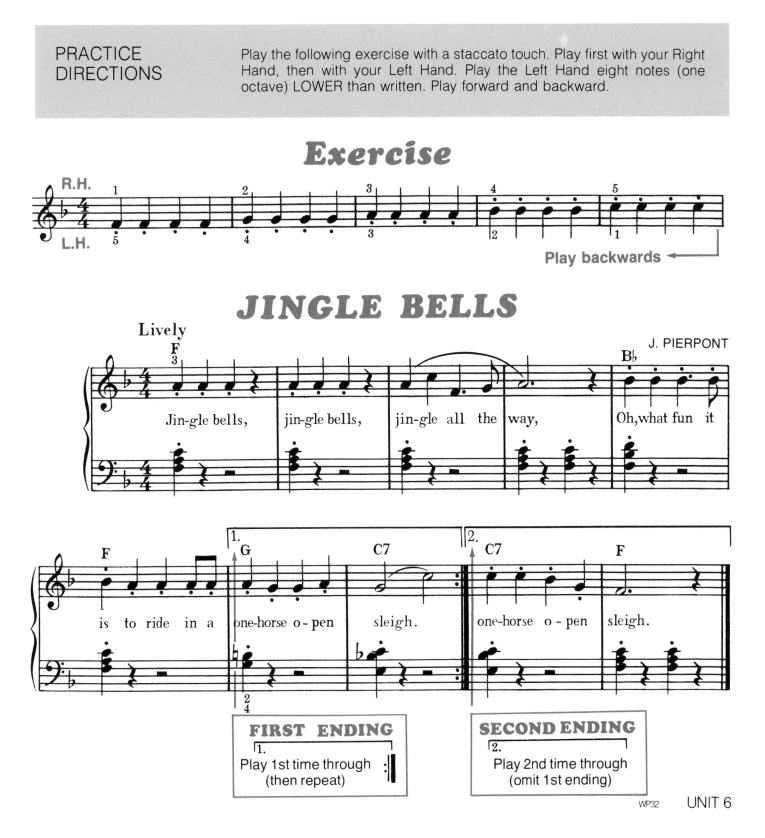

Exercise

Play backwards ←

JINGLE BELLS

J. PIERPONT

Lively

Jin-gle bells, jin-gle bells, jin-gle all the way, Oh, what fun it

is to ride in a one-horse o-pen sleigh. one-horse o-pen sleigh.

FIRST ENDING
1.
Play 1st time through
(then repeat)

SECOND ENDING
2.
Play 2nd time through
(omit 1st ending)

GROUP 1 KEYS (CHORDS)

You have learned to play in three keys: C, G, and F. These three keys are called the GROUP 1 KEYS because they all have the SAME feel and look in their I chords. All three I chords are formed with WHITE keys.

"white — white — white"

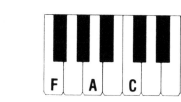

BLOCK CHORD · BROKEN CHORD

Notes of a chord played at the same time form a BLOCK CHORD:

Notes of a chord played one-at-a-time form a BROKEN CHORD:

CHANGING HAND POSITIONS

When playing the C, G, and F chords with the same hand, you must MOVE your hand for each new chord. This is called CHANGING HAND POSITIONS.

PRACTICE DIRECTIONS	Practice the following **Chord Progression** using the Group 1 chords. Think ahead for each new hand position.

Chord Progression

Block chord   **Broken chord**

You are ready to begin a new book in the **OLDER BEGINNER PIANO LIBRARY — Religious Favorites.**

© 1978 KJOS WEST, San Diego, California (Ed. No. WP41)

GROUP 1 KEYS (FIVE FINGER POSITIONS)

In the Group 1 Keys the five finger position for C and G have the same feel and look. The pattern for these keys is:

"white — white — white — white — white"

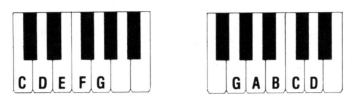

F is the UNUSUAL key in Group 1 because the five finger pattern is:

"white — white — white — **black** — white"

| PRACTICE DIRECTIONS | Practice the following **ETUDE*** made from the Group 1 five finger positions. Think ahead for the hand position changes. |

ETUDE

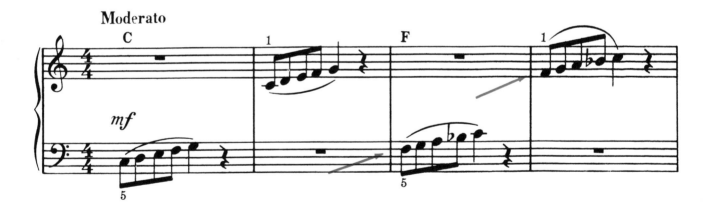

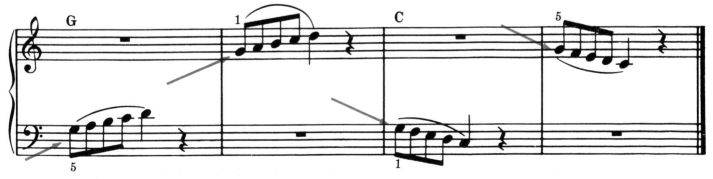

*Etude is a French word meaning STUDY or EXERCISE.

PRACTICE DIRECTIONS

Practice the following **CHORD ETUDE** which uses the Group 1 chords. Notice the use of both block chords and broken chords. Think ahead for the hand position changes.

CHORD ETUDE

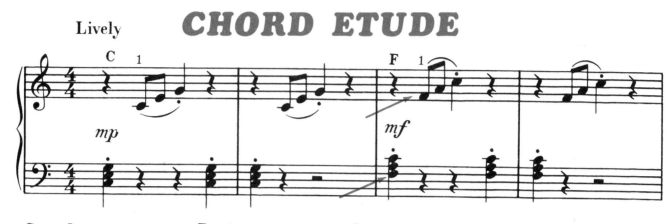

PRACTICE DIRECTIONS

Think ahead for the hand position changes.

ETUDE IN BLUE

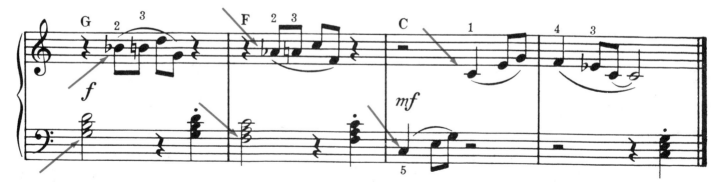

You are ready to begin a new book in the **OLDER BEGINNER PIANO LIBRARY — Favorite Melodies the World Over, Level 1.**

©1977 KJOS WEST, San Diego, California. (Ed. No. WP37)

CRESCENDO	DIMINUENDO
gradually play louder	gradually play softer

PRACTICE DIRECTIONS

Look through **THE BLUES** before playing it. Write in the hand position (chord) names. Draw arrows up or down for the changes in hand positions.

THE BLUES *

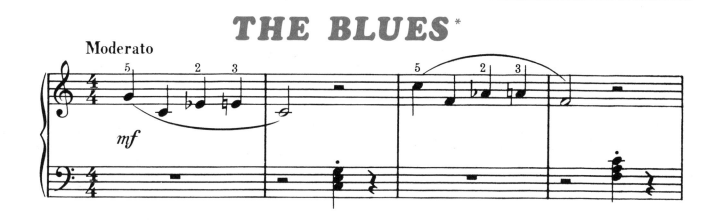

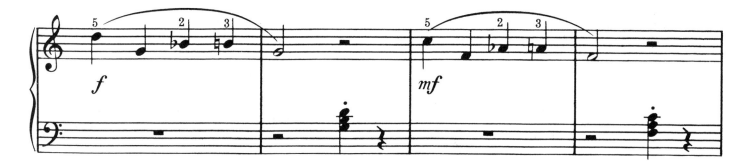

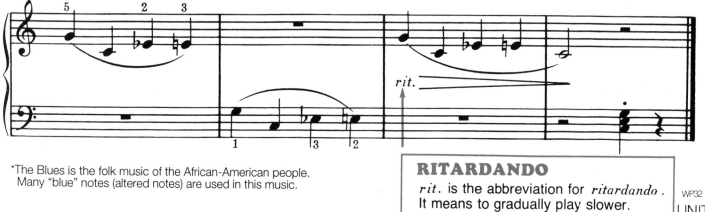

*The Blues is the folk music of the African-American people. Many "blue" notes (altered notes) are used in this music.

RITARDANDO

rit. is the abbreviation for *ritardando*. It means to gradually play slower.

WP32

UNIT 6

ACCENT SIGN >

This sign > is called an ACCENT. It means to stress or ACCENT a note. Play LOUDER when you see an accent sign. An accent may also be used for a group of notes:

Play:

TECHNIC
(GROUP 1 KEY FIVE FINGER PATTERNS)

PRACTICE DIRECTIONS

Look through **LITTLE ROCK** before playing it. Circle the broken chords. Write in the chord names. Draw arrows up or down for the changes in hand positions.

LITTLE ROCK *

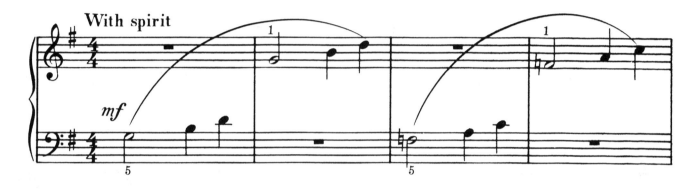

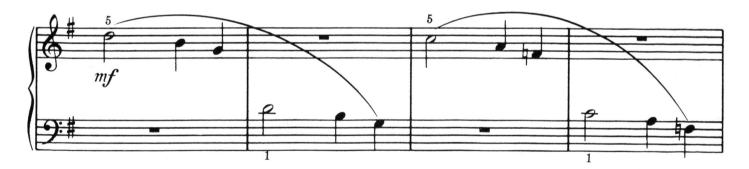

*Rock is a form of popular music in which pounding rhythms are featured. Usually accents are featured elements in rock music.

WP32   UNIT 6

REVIEW · UNIT 6

1. Write the I chords in the Group 1 keys. Play them.

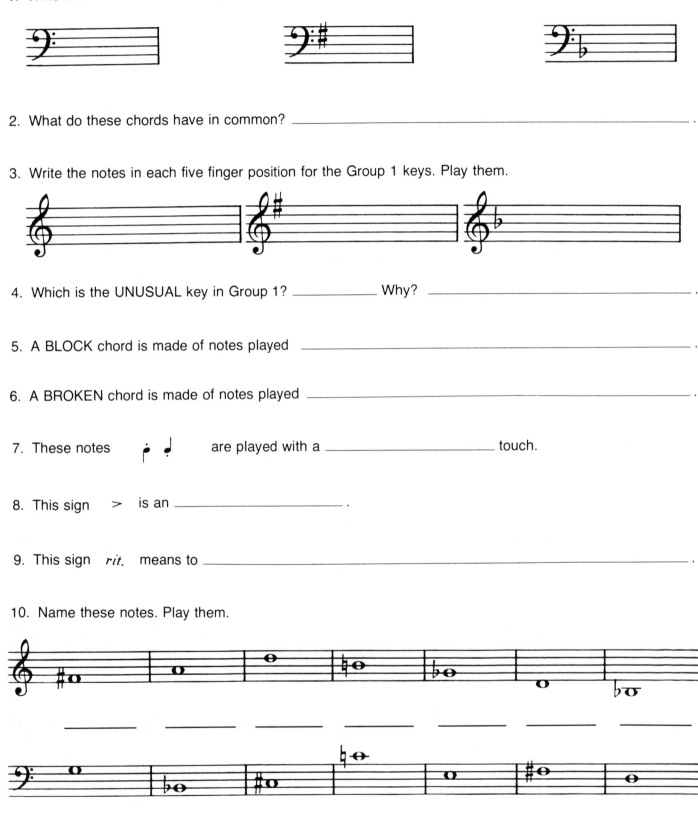

2. What do these chords have in common? _____ .

3. Write the notes in each five finger position for the Group 1 keys. Play them.

4. Which is the UNUSUAL key in Group 1? _____ Why? _____ .

5. A BLOCK chord is made of notes played _____ .

6. A BROKEN chord is made of notes played _____ .

7. These notes ♩ ♩ are played with a _____ touch.

8. This sign > is an _____ .

9. This sign *rit.* means to _____ .

10. Name these notes. Play them.

UNIT 7

- HALF STEPS AND WHOLE STEPS
- C MAJOR SCALE
- SCALE PREPARATION DRILLS
- SCALE MELODIES

LITTLE BIT OF ROCK

Moderately fast rock beat

You are ready to begin a new book — **Pop, Rock, 'N Blues, Book 1.**

HALF STEPS AND WHOLE STEPS

HALF STEP

From one key to the nearest key with NO KEY IN BETWEEN is a HALF STEP.

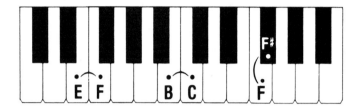

HALF STEPS (1/2)

WHOLE STEP

From one key to a neighbor key with ONE KEY IN BETWEEN is a WHOLE STEP.

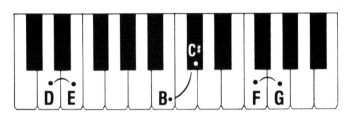

WHOLE STEPS (1)

C MAJOR SCALE

HOW MAJOR SCALES ARE FORMED

The word SCALE comes from a Latin word meaning LADDER. A scale has tones (like steps on a ladder) which go up and down. There are eight tones in a Major scale. The tones are called scale DEGREES. The scale degrees are arranged in the pattern of WHOLE STEPS (1) and HALF STEPS (1/2) shown below.

C MAJOR SCALE

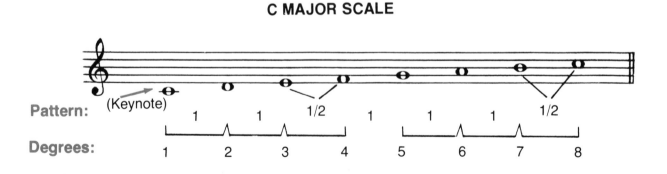

SCALE PREPARATION DRILLS

TURNING THE THUMB UNDER

PRACTICE DIRECTIONS	Practice these drills for turning the THUMB UNDER. Play the Right Hand drill first, then the Left Hand. Play each drill several times. Practice SLOWLY at first.

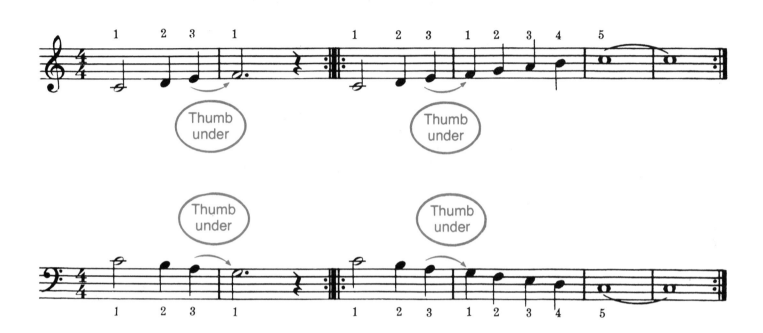

CROSSING OVER THE THUMB

PRACTICE DIRECTIONS	Practice these drills for crossing OVER THE THUMB. Play the Right Hand drill first, then the Left Hand. Play each drill several times. Practice SLOWLY at first.

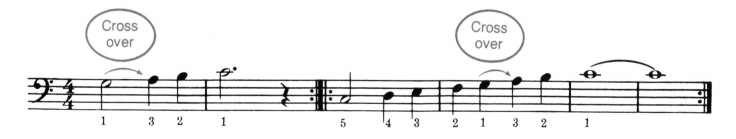

SCALE MELODIES

PRACTICE DIRECTIONS	Many songs use scales in their melodies. Several Christmas songs are given below. Play each song, first with your Right Hand, then with your Left Hand. Play the Left Hand eight scale degrees (one octave) LOWER than written.

TIME SIGNATURE $\quad C = \frac{4}{4}$

The sign C is another way of indicating the $\frac{4}{4}$ time signature. This sign is called COMMON TIME.

C MAJOR SCALE ETUDE

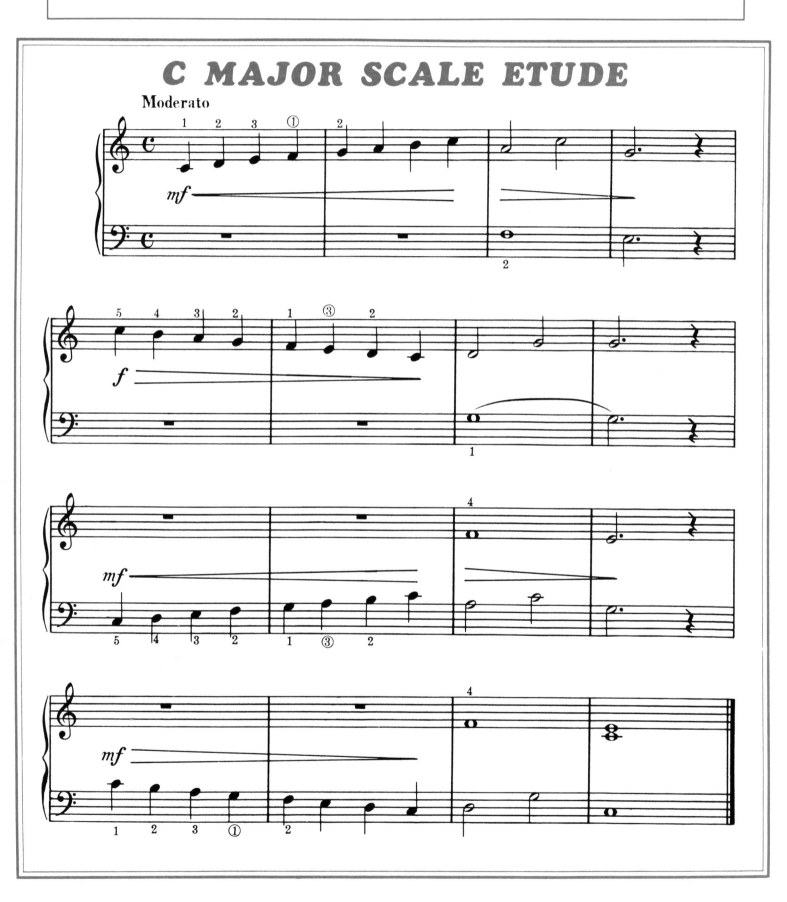

TIME SIGNATURE ₵ = 2/2

This sign ₵ means ALLA BREVE (or "Cut Time"). There are TWO strong beats to the measure. When you first play in Cut Time, count **4/4** time (4 beats to the measure). Then, when you know the piece better, count **2/2** time (2 beats to the measure).

CARELESS LOVE

SHE WORE A YELLOW RIBBON

Lively march tempo

TRADITIONAL

Round her neck she wore a yel-low rib-bon, She wore it in the spring-time and in the month of May, And if you asked her why she al-ways wore it, She'd tell you for her lov-er who was far, far a-way.

Chorus

Far a-way, far a-way, She'd tell you for her lov-er who was far, far a-way. way.

REVIEW · UNIT 7

1. Write 1/2 under the half steps shown on this keyboard.

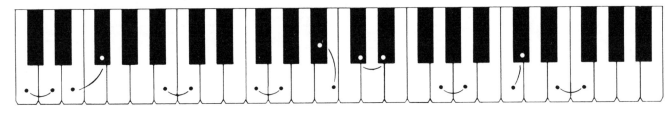

___ ___ ___ ___ ___ ___ ___ ___ ___

2. Write 1 under the whole steps shown on this keyboard.

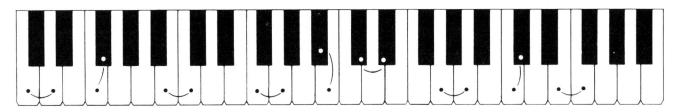

___ ___ ___ ___ ___ ___ ___

3. How many tones are there in a Major scale? _____ .

4. The tones are called scale _____ .

5. Mark the whole (1) and half (1/2) steps in this C Major scale.

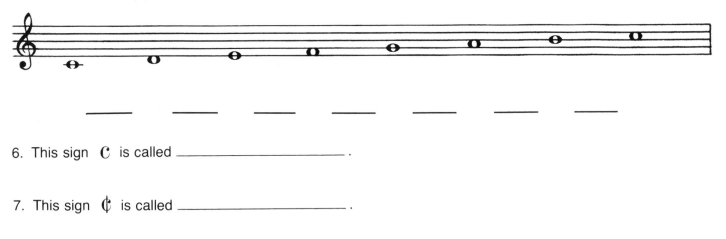

___ ___ ___ ___ ___ ___ ___

6. This sign C is called _____ .

7. This sign ¢ is called _____ .

UNIT 8

- **G MAJOR SCALE**
- **⁶⁄₈ TIME SIGNATURE**

GOIN' HOME

Largo (very slowly)

ANTONIN DVOŘÁK (1841-1904)

© 1922 Oliver Ditson Company
Adapted and Reprinted By Permission Of The Publisher
Theodore Presser Company

G MAJOR SCALE

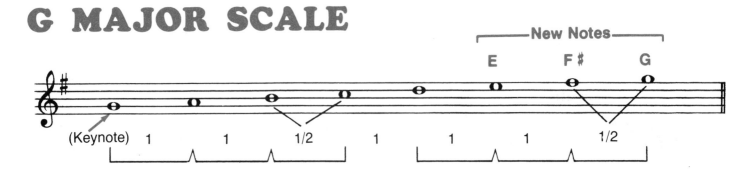

Two Scale Studies

1.

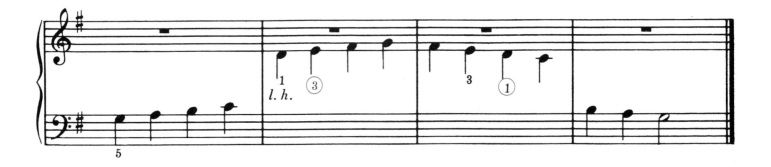

2.

Contrary Motion

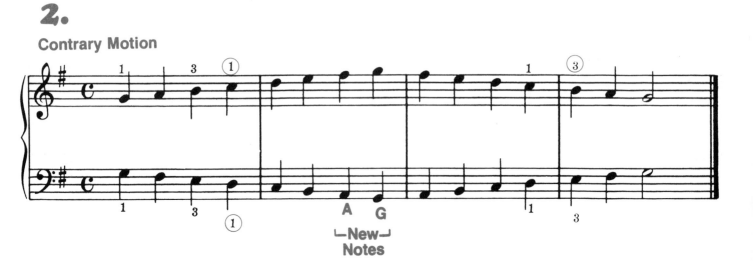

G MAJOR SCALE ETUDE

6/8 TIME SIGNATURE

All time signatures have two numbers. The UPPER NUMBER tells how many BEATS there are IN A MEASURE. The LOWER NUMBER tells the KIND OF NOTE THAT GETS ONE BEAT.

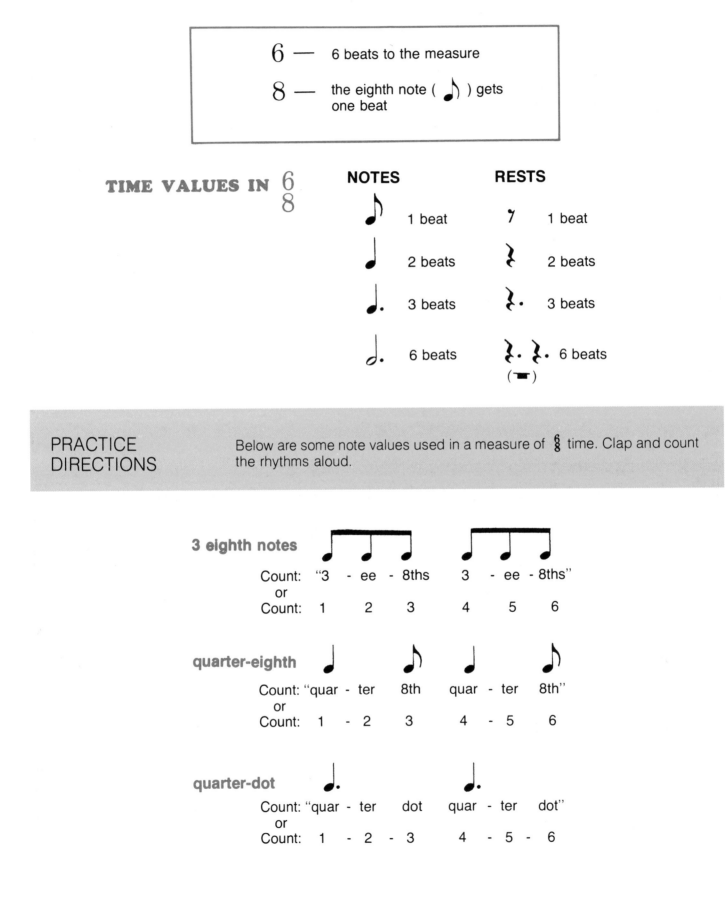

6 — 6 beats to the measure

8 — the eighth note (♪) gets one beat

TIME VALUES IN 6/8

NOTES		RESTS	
♪	1 beat	＇	1 beat
♩	2 beats	ξ	2 beats
♩.	3 beats	ξ·	3 beats
♩.	6 beats	ξ· ξ· (▬)	6 beats

PRACTICE DIRECTIONS — Below are some note values used in a measure of 6/8 time. Clap and count the rhythms aloud.

3 eighth notes

Count: "3 - ee - 8ths   3 - ee - 8ths"
or
Count: 1   2   3   4   5   6

quarter-eighth

Count: "quar - ter   8th   quar - ter   8th"
or
Count: 1 - 2   3   4 - 5   6

quarter-dot

Count: "quar - ter   dot   quar - ter   dot"
or
Count: 1 - 2 - 3   4 - 5 - 6

Clap and count the rhythm aloud BEFORE playing each piece. Then play and count the rhythm aloud.

ROW, ROW, ROW YOUR BOAT

Lively

mf

Row, row, row your boat, Gen - tly down the stream.___

Mer - ri - ly, mer - ri - ly, mer - ri - ly, mer - ri - ly, Life is but a dream.___

TWO ETUDES IN 6/8 TIME

1. Moderato

f-p

2. Moderato

f-p

Low G

Clap and count the rhythm to each of the following songs BEFORE playing them.

IT CAME UPON THE MIDNIGHT CLEAR

RICHARD S. WILLIS

THE MAN ON THE FLYING TRAPEZE

TRADITIONAL

CIELITO LINDO
(BEAUTIFUL HEAVEN)

MEXICAN FOLK SONG

REVIEW · UNIT 8

1. Mark the whole (1) and half steps (½) in the G Major scale.

_____ _____ _____ _____ _____ _____ _____

2. Write these key signatures in both clefs.

G Major   C Major   F Major

3. In $\frac{6}{8}$ time write the number of beats these notes receive.

_____ _____ _____ _____

4. Draw rests which correspond to the notes in Number 3 above.

_____ _____ _____ _____

5. Play the following chord progression with your Left Hand. Use the rhythm indicated.

UNIT 9

- **F MAJOR SCALE**
- **THE ORDER OF SHARPS**
- **MAJOR SHARP KEY SIGNATURES**
- **GROUP 2 KEYS**
- **READING IN D MAJOR**
- **READING IN A MAJOR**
- **READING IN E MAJOR**

F MAJOR SCALE

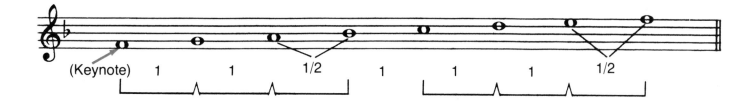

(Keynote)   1   1   1/2   1   1   1   1/2

PRACTICE DIRECTIONS	Practice the F Major scale first with your Right Hand, then with your Left Hand.

Note the different fingering in the RIGHT HAND: 1   2   3   4   1   2   3   4

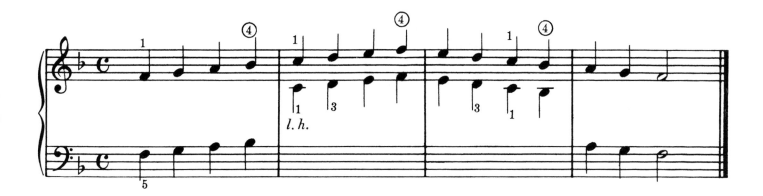

THE ORDER OF SHARPS

The SHARPS are ALWAYS written in the same order on the staff. MEMORIZE this order.

Line Sharp

Space Sharp

F C G D A E B

| PRACTICE DIRECTIONS | Write the order of sharps three times on this staff. |

MAJOR SHARP KEY SIGNATURES *

The KEY SIGNATURE at the beginning of each staff tells you:
1) which notes to play sharped or flatted THROUGHOUT the piece
   and
2) the main tonality or KEY of the piece.

RULES FOR FINDING SHARP KEY SIGNATURES

1) name the LAST sharp to the right then

   D Major

2) name the NEXT letter in the musical alphabet (go UP a half step). This is the name of the MAJOR KEY.

| PRACTICE DIRECTIONS | Name these keys. |

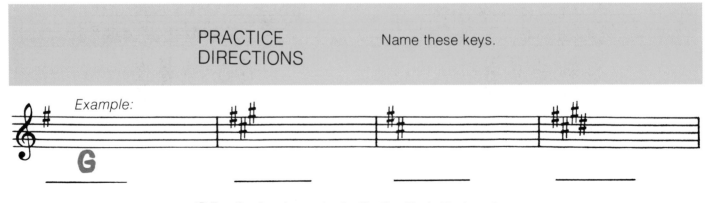

Example:

G

*Drill on the sharp keys using the **Bastien Music Flashcards.***

GROUP 2 KEYS

<table>
<tr><td>

GROUP 2 KEYS   **D, A, E**

The GROUP 2 KEYS (D, A, E) have a BLACK KEY under the MIDDLE FINGER and white keys on either side in their I or tonic chords. E is underlined because it is the UNUSUAL key in this group. The five finger position in E has TWO black keys under the 2nd and 3rd fingers in the Right Hand, and under the 3rd and 4th fingers in the Left Hand.

</td></tr>
</table>

POSITIONS FOR THE GROUP 2 KEYS

> **PRACTICE DIRECTIONS**   The circled finger numbers outline the I or tonic chords within the five finger positions below. Play these five finger positions and I chords. MEMORIZE them.

KEY OF D

LEFT HAND   **RIGHT HAND**

KEY OF A

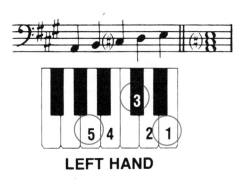
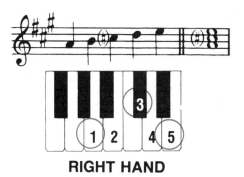

LEFT HAND   **RIGHT HAND**

KEY OF E

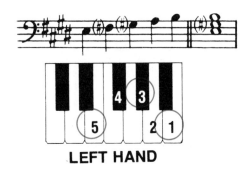

LEFT HAND   **RIGHT HAND**

READING IN D MAJOR

| PRACTICE DIRECTIONS | Practice the five finger position and the primary chords in D Major BEFORE playing the three pieces on this page. |

1.

2.

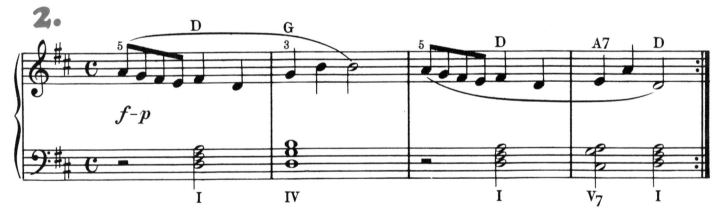

3.

*The D Major scale is given on page 95.

**The primary chords are the I, IV, V7 chords of a key.

KUM-BA-YA

Moderately

FOLK ANTHEM

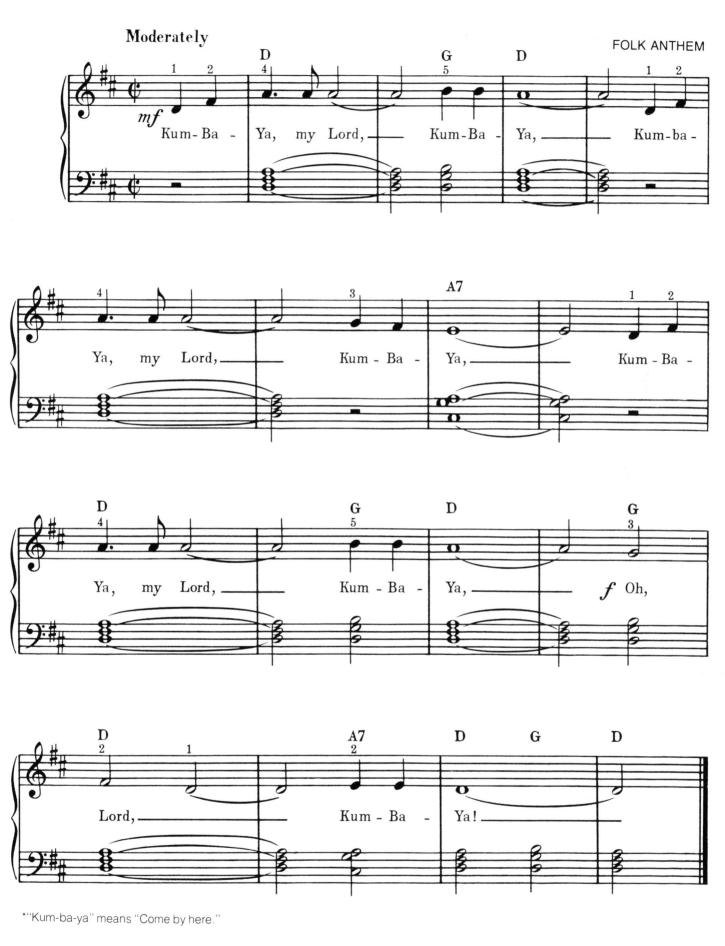

*"Kum-ba-ya" means "Come by here."

READING IN A MAJOR

1.

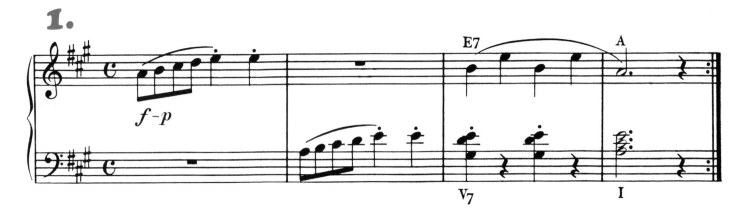

2.

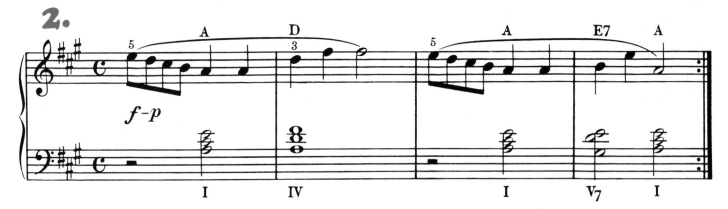

3.

*The A Major scale is given on page 95.

THEME
(FROM MOZART'S "SONATA IN A")

WOLFGANG AMADEUS MOZART (1756-1791)

READING IN E MAJOR

Practice the five finger position and the primary chords in E Major BEFORE playing the three pieces on this page.

1.

2.

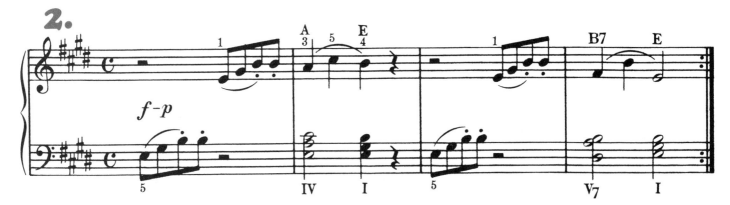

3.

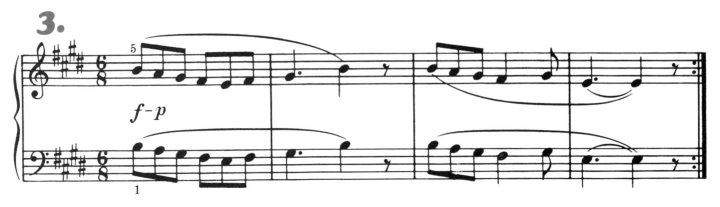

*The E Major scale is given on page 95.

THE BIG ROCK CANDY MOUNTAINS

FOLK SONG

Oh, the buzz-ing of the bees in the cig-a-rette trees by the

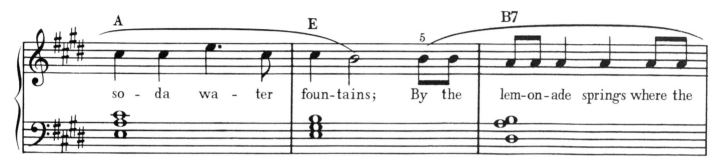

so - da wa - ter foun-tains; By the lem-on-ade springs where the

mock-ing bird sings in the Big Rock Can - dy Moun-tains.

EIGHT O'CLOCK ROCK

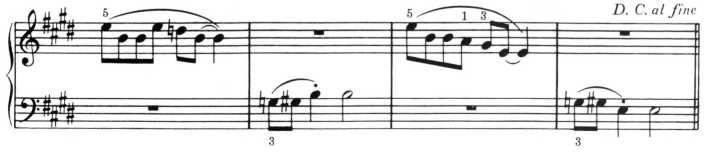

REVIEW - UNIT 9

1. Mark the whole (1) and half (1/2) steps in the F Major scale.

2. The order of sharps is ____ ____ ____ ____ ____ ____ ____ .

3. Name these Major key signatures.

_____   _____   _____   _____

4. Write the I chords in the Group 2 keys. Play them.

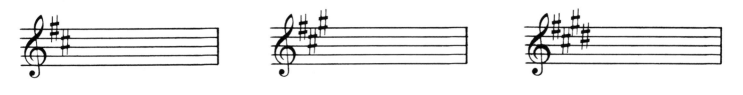

5. What do they have in common? _____ .

6. Write the notes in each five finger position for the Group 2 keys. Play them.

7. Which is the unusual key in Group 2? _____ Why? _____ .

UNIT 10

- **THE DAMPER PEDAL**
- **MINOR CHORDS**

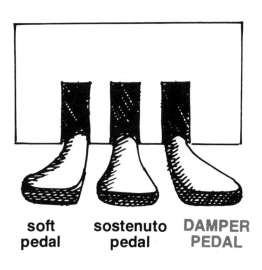

soft pedal   sostenuto pedal   DAMPER PEDAL

THE DAMPER PEDAL

The pedal to the RIGHT is called the DAMPER PEDAL. When pressed, the dampers lift from the strings to allow the strings to vibrate freely. Thus, the damper pedal is used to sustain notes. The damper is the pedal used most often on the piano.

PEDAL TECHNIC

Press the damper pedal with your RIGHT foot.
Keep your HEEL on the FLOOR when you use the pedal.

Press   **Hold**   **Lift**

PRACTICE DIRECTIONS	Practice this exercise BEFORE using the pedal in your music.

PEDAL ETUDE

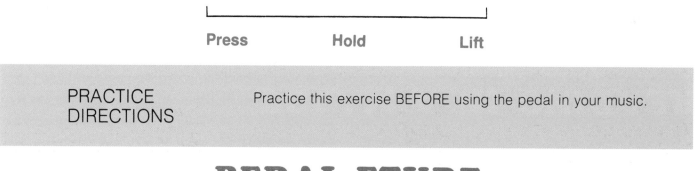

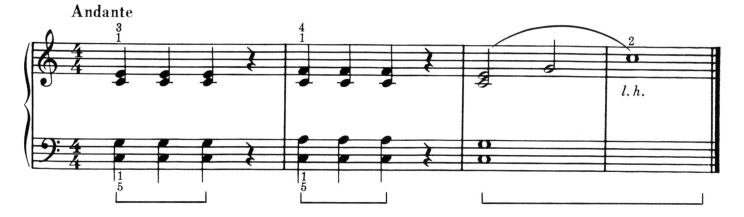

OVER THE WAVES

JUVENTINO ROSAS

Medium waltz tempo

MINOR CHORDS

To form a minor chord (or a minor five finger position), begin with a Major chord and move your MIDDLE FINGER DOWN to the nearest key (a half step). The nearest key may be either black or white.

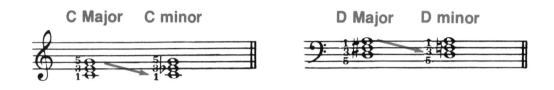

PRACTICE DIRECTIONS
Practice the following Major, minor chord drill. Play first with your Right Hand, then with your Left Hand. Play the Left Hand eight scale degrees (one octave) LOWER than written. Play the chords by "feel." Do NOT look at your hand for the chord changes.

Transpose: F, G, D, A, E

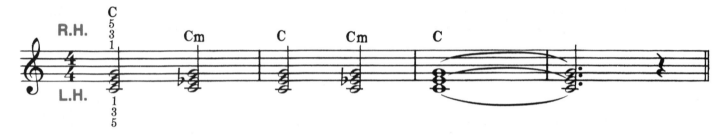

THE ERIE CANAL

Transpose: C, F, G, A, E minor
Key of D minor

W.S. ALLEN

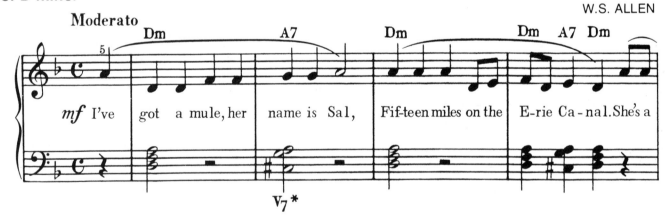

*NOTE: The V7 chord is the SAME for both Major and minor keys.

UNIT 10   WP32

PRACTICE DIRECTIONS — Practice playing these leger line and space notes BEFORE playing *MARCH SLAV.*

Preparatory Drill

MARCH SLAV

Key of A minor

Moderato

PETER ILYITCH TCHAIKOVSKY (1840-1893)

WP32 UNIT 10

OCTAVE SIGN *8va* ----------- ⌐

The OCTAVE sign means to play eight scale degrees (one octave) higher or lower than written. Play one octave HIGHER when the sign is placed ABOVE notes. Play one octave LOWER when the sign is placed BELOW notes.

THE ENTERTAINER

SCOTT JOPLIN
arranged by James Bastien

REVIEW · UNIT 10

1. Name these Major key signatures.

　　　＿＿＿＿　　　＿＿＿＿　　　＿＿＿＿　　　＿＿＿＿　　　＿＿＿＿

2. To form a minor chord, the ＿＿＿＿＿＿＿＿＿＿＿ note must be lowered a half step.

3. Name these minor chords. Play them.

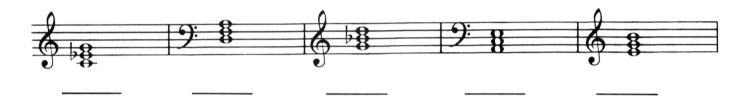

　　＿＿＿＿　　　＿＿＿＿　　　＿＿＿＿　　　＿＿＿＿　　　＿＿＿＿

4. In both Major and minor keys, the V7 chord is the ＿＿＿＿＿＿＿＿＿＿＿

5. Play these chord progressions.

a.

b.

c.

SUPPLEMENTARY REPERTOIRE

MELODY IN F

ANTON RUBINSTEIN
arranged by James Bastien

DANUBE WAVES

Key of A minor

JAN IVANOVICI
arranged by James Bastien

SUPPLEMENTARY REPERTOIRE

SWAN LAKE
(THEME)

Key of D minor

PETER TCHAIKOVSKY
arranged by James Bastien

MARIONETTE'S FUNERAL MARCH

Key of D minor

Strict march tempo

CHARLES GOUNOD
arranged by James Bastien

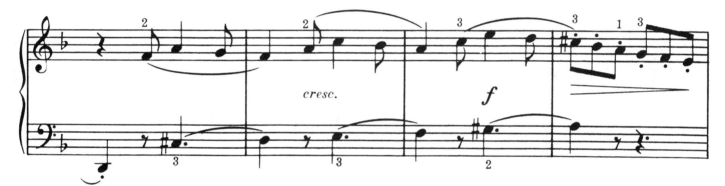

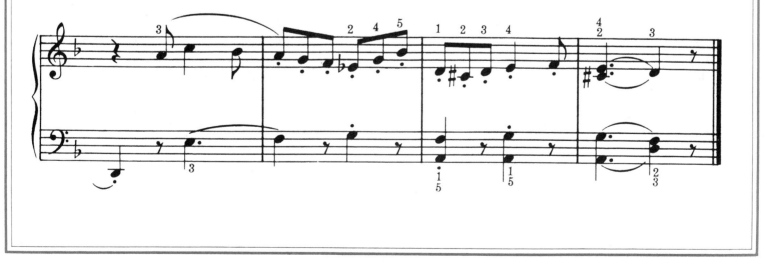

HUGARIAN DANCE NO. 5

Key of A minor

Allegro moderato

Johannes Brahms
arranged by James Bastien

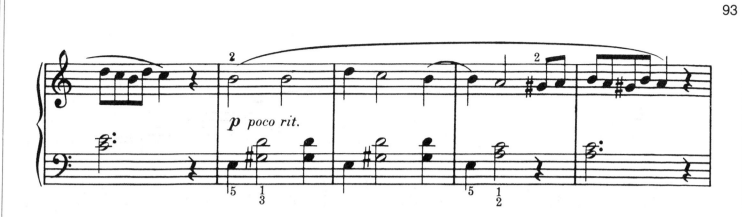

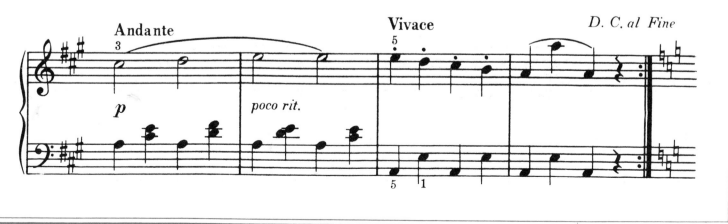

RUSSIAN DANCE
(FROM "THE NUTCRACKER SUITE")

PETER TCHAIKOVSKY
arranged by James Bastien

Vivace

REFERENCE
PRIMARY CHORDS

PRACTICE DIRECTIONS

Practice the following chord progression in C Major. Notice that you move fingers $\frac{5}{3}$ UP for the IV chord. Repeat this progression until you can play it smoothly. Play by "feel." Do NOT look at your hand for the chord changes. Use the CORRECT fingering. MEMORIZE this chord progression.

Transpose: G, F

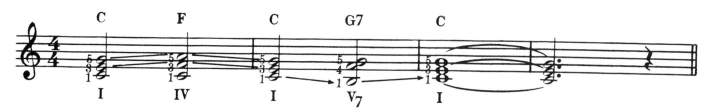

MAJOR SCALES OF D, A, E

D Major

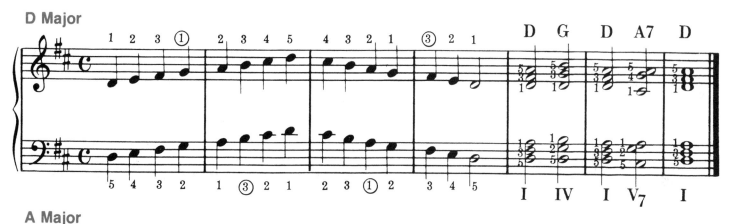

A Major

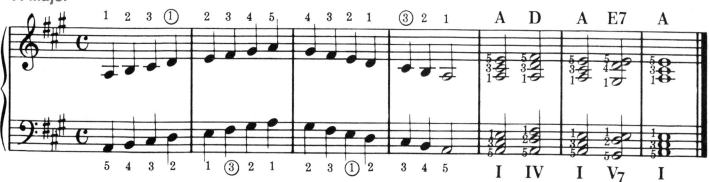

E Major

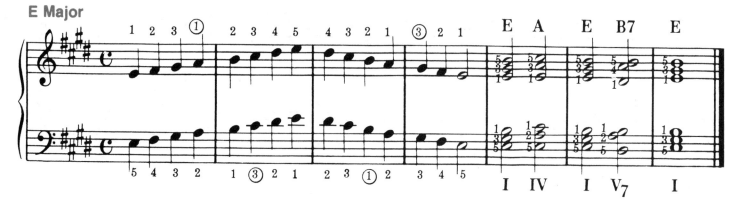

MUSIC DICTIONARY

TERM	ABBREVIATION or SIGN	MEANING
Accent Sign	>	stress and play louder
Alla Breve		$\frac{2}{2}$ time; two strong beats to the measure
Allegretto		moderately fast
Allegro		fast ("cheerful")
Andante		walking speed
A tempo		return to the original speed
Common Time	C	another way of indicating $\frac{4}{4}$ time
Crescendo	cresc.	gradually play louder
Da Capo al Fine	D. C. al Fine	return to the beginning and play to the word "Fine"
Decrescendo	decresc.	gradually play softer
Dal Segno al Fine	D. S. al Fine	return to the sign (𝄋) and play to the word "Fine"
Diminuendo	dim.	gradually play softer
Fermata	𝄐	hold the note (or notes) longer
Fine	Fine	the end
Forte	f	loud
Fortissimo	ff	very loud
Largo		very slowly
Legato		smooth, connected tones
Mezzo Forte	mf	moderately loud
Mezzo Piano	mp	moderately soft
Moderato		a moderate speed
Octave Sign	8va	play eight scale degrees (one octave) higher when the sign is above the notes; play eight scale degrees lower when the sign is below the notes
Pianissimo	pp	very soft
Piano	p	soft
Repeat Sign		go back and play again
Ritardando	rit.	gradually play slower
Simile		similar
Staccato		short, disconnected tones
Tempo		rate of speed
Tie		connects notes on the same line or space; hold the notes for their combined value
Vivace		lively